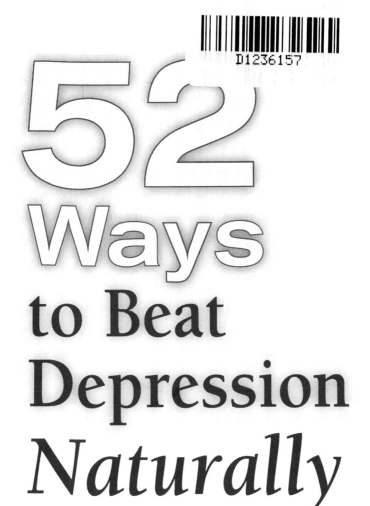

52 Ways to Beat Depression Naturally

INDIGORIVER
PUBLISHING

52
Ways
to Beat
Depression
Naturally

Nicole McCance M.A., C.Psych.Assoc

52 Ways to Beat Depression Naturally

Editors: Adam Tillinghast, Matthew Jordan, Donna Melillo
Cover Design: Randy Hamilton / Hamilton Art Agency / hamiltonartagency.com
Interior Design and Layout: Rick Soldin / book-comp.com
Research and Writing Assistance: Amanda Paterson
Administrative Support: Angie Doyle

Indigo River Publishing
3 West Garden Street Ste. 352
Pensacola, FL 32502
www.indigoriverpublishing.com

Ordering Information:
Quantity sales: Special discounts are available on quantity purchases by corporations, associations, and others. For details, contact the publisher at the address above.

Orders by U.S. trade bookstores and wholesalers: Please contact the publisher at the address above.

Printed in the United States of America

Library of Congress Control Number: 2013930405
ISBN 978-0-9856033-7-3

First Edition

With Indigo River Publishing, you can always expect great books, strong voices, and meaningful messages. Most importantly, you'll always find ... words worth reading.

This book is dedicated to my dad, Steve. Thanks for always being proud of me and helping me believe in myself.

Contents

1 There is Light at the End of the Tunnel!

"Most of the important things in the world have been accomplished by people who have kept on trying when there seemed to be no hope at all."

—Dale Carnegie

Are you sick of feeling empty inside? Are you sick of being on edge and irritable? Are you sick of feeling like *everything requires extra effort?* Do you feel that you have changed for the worse? Are you no longer your old self? Have others noticed a change in you? Has your doctor or another healthcare professional advised that you may be suffering from depression?

If you answered yes to any of the questions above, you are not alone. Depression is an all-encompassing illness—one that affects the body, the nervous system, mood, thoughts, and behaviors. The reach of depression is astounding; if you don't suffer from it, the chance that you know someone who does is very high.

If you are one of the millions suffering from depression, you are holding a virtual toolbox in your hands. If you use this toolbox, you will start to feel better—I promise. It is possible to get back to the old you. In fact, you have not changed! I often hear from my clients that they feel they no longer recognize themselves—that they used to be "happy go lucky" and loved life, but now they can barely get through the day. They are confused and scared and not sure what has happened to them. They feel like they are stuck in a dark hole and are having difficulty getting out by themselves.

The good news is that I can help you emerge from that dark hole and find yourself … joyful and self-confident again.

Before we get started, it is good to ask yourself, "Am I ready for a change?" This book is about taking action. If you take the steps I recommend in this book, you will feel better. But you have to be committed. Are you ready for something different? Are you ready to get back to the old you?

After reading this book, **you will feel different** because you will have learned skills to target your specific symptoms of depression. **You are unique, and your depression is unique**. The exercises that work for one person may not always work for another. This book offers a variety of tools, and you can choose the ones that work for you. Once you find a tip effective, you can incorporate it into your life.

Throughout the book, you'll find helpful icons which will indicate the ease with which a particular tip can be adopted. The icons work as shown on the next page.

If you're not sure how best to incorporate these techniques on your own, and if you want a more guided structure, you can find several helpful, detailed schedules to follow in the back of this book.

3 icons appear with each tip to let you know what type of tip you can expect

WHEN TO DO   HOW LONG   WHAT's NEEDED

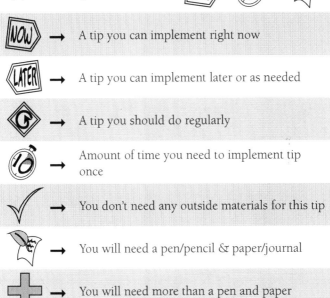

→ A tip you can implement right now

→ A tip you can implement later or as needed

→ A tip you should do regularly

→ Amount of time you need to implement tip once

→ You don't need any outside materials for this tip

→ You will need a pen/pencil & paper/journal

→ You will need more than a pen and paper

As a psychotherapist, I am a true believer in teaching my clients, and now my readers, natural ways to combat depression, instead of relying only on pharmaceuticals. Natural techniques may take longer to produce results than medication; but when you learn natural techniques, exercises, and concrete tools to overcome your depression, those skills will stay with you forever. You do not need a prescription to receive these gifts, and you are getting my expertise, supported by research.

When you continue to practice these exercises, you will start to feel lighter in your body, and you will start to feel relief from the sadness in your heart and mind. Eventually, with practice, these tips will help you to have hope again and help you to wake up in the morning feeling good and looking forward to your day.

I am sharing the 52 best ways to naturally overcome depression with you in the hope that you will begin your journey to a better life ... starting now.

How Do You Know if You are Depressed?

It is helpful to meet with a clinician, such as a family doctor, psychologist, or psychiatrist, who can discuss your symptoms and properly diagnose you. Depressive symptoms can often be tied to other disorders, including a thyroid condition, so it is important not to mistake your feelings with a medical issue. To begin, simply complete the brief assessment of your depressed symptoms on the facing page. Later, after you've incorporated a majority of the tips in this book (for a period of at least 30 days), you can track your progress using the same questionnaire. (You can find a full page version of this assessment on page 123.)

If you answered *yes* to any combination of the questions, you may suffer from depression.

[Remember your age and physical health may actually account for some of the answers above, and may be due to other factors besides depression. If you have questions, talk to your family doctor to confirm your condition.]

The key is frequency and intensity. If you're experiencing a heavy toll of symptoms every day for a period of at least 2 weeks without relief, it is very likely that you're suffering from depression.

Symptoms of Clinical Depression

Self-Assessment   Date: _____

Yes No

☐   ☐   Do you feel depressed or sad for most of the day, or every day?

☐   ☐   Have you lost interest in all or almost all of the activities you used to enjoy?

☐   ☐   Have you lost or gained a significant amount of weight, or has your appetite changed dramatically?

☐   ☐   Do you often have trouble sleeping, or do you sleep all the time?

☐   ☐   Do you feel restless or agitated frequently?

☐   ☐   Is your energy level low and/or do you feel fatigued?

☐   ☐   Do you have feelings of inadequacy, loss of self-esteem, and/or do you put yourself down?

☐   ☐   Do you have trouble concentrating, paying attention, or thinking clearly?

☐   ☐   Do you have recurring thoughts of death or suicide or sometimes wish you were dead?

The severity and types of symptoms vary from individual to individual, of course; and even if you're coping with milder symptoms, you can benefit greatly from the tips in this book.

Now that you are aware of the extent of your depressive symptoms, you are ready to reduce them, and finally, overcome them. You can start out slowly by trying just one tip each day. As you feel more motivated, try two or three tips each day. Most of all, keep trying, whether you are discouraged or not.

Materials/People You Will Need for this Journey

A notebook or journal and a pen or pencil.

Purchase a notebook in a nice color or pattern, one that you find soothing and inviting. It does not matter if it is from the dollar store, as long as you have paper to put down your thoughts. I suggest that you record your thoughts and feelings in your journal and complete the exercises in this book.

Think about your family and friends. Select one or two that you believe would be uplifting and supportive. Ask them if they would be willing to help you through this process, if needed. If you don't have a friend or family member close by, look up a group that you can join online. **It's important for you to have a *support person* through this process.**

To connect with individuals who are also going through similar issues, I recommend visiting an online forum like www.depressionforums.org. Remember, you are not alone.

You also need a willingness to read these tips and implement them into your life. That is it!

2 Tips to Calm You

"Trust the Process"

Tip #1

Diaphragmatic Breathing

In times of emotional distress, the nervous system jumps into a higher gear and causes a number of physiological responses. We can begin to sweat, our muscles tighten, and our heart rate increases. You may notice that when you feel particularly anxious or distressed, your breathing quickens and your chest heaves up and down.

However, you can fight these responses just by consciously changing your breathing patterns. Studies have shown that the way we breathe is central to our ability to ease stress. By practicing diaphragmatic breathing, you influence the body and cause it to relax. You can interrupt the anxious response you are feeling; and once you master this technique, you should be able to calm your nervous system in just a few minutes.

Try This!

- First, remove yourself from the stressful situation, whether it is a disagreement with a friend, family member, co-worker, or another stressor. Move to a quiet room like a bedroom or office.
- Sit or lie down.
- Place your palms flat on your abdomen just below your rib cage.
- Close your eyes and start to focus on your breathing. Imagine an invisible barrier around your body, and any stress from the external world simply bouncing off of that wall. Think only of your breathing.

- Inhale through your nose and think about the flow of air into your body. Count to 3 slowly each time you inhale, and again, count to 3 as you exhale.
- Imagine that there is a balloon in your abdomen, and as you inhale, the air causes the balloon to expand. As you exhale, the balloon deflates.

Be sure to take slow breaths, but do not inhale to the point that you feel uncomfortable. This should be a relaxing process. If you feel dizzy or experience pain, return to your normal breathing pattern for a few minutes and try again. You may have been breathing too quickly or too deeply.

Practice this for a few minutes each day; and over the course of a week, you should be able to call upon this breathing technique any time to instantly reduce your stress.

For a free breathing technique download, visit
www.nicolemccance.com.

Anger Releasing Techniques

Think about the word emotion. Think of E as energy, and Motion as the movement of energy in the body. When I meet with clients, I can see that they hold anger in their body as people clench their jaws or fists, grind their teeth, or experience muscle tension. If you don't release your anger, you harm yourself and you will start to behave aggressively toward others.

I suggest to my clients, and anyone holding anger in their body, to release it. There are several techniques you can use to do this.

Try This!

○ One way to release anger is to use your voice. You might be nervous or embarrassed to make noise, because it draws attention. However, you can turn up a good song and sing loudly in your car without anyone knowing. You can also sing in the shower if no one is home (or even if they are). Singing helps to get rid of tension in the body and replaces it with the positive feeling that listening to a great song brings.

○ Release emotion by yelling. Feel the air coming from your gut and visualize the angry feelings leaving your body with your breath. You can do this in your car, into a pillow, or at home. If you are nervous about being heard, screaming into a pillow is a great tool.

○ Take a pillow and beat your bed or couch with it. Literally hit the bed multiple times with the pillow. If you feel like it, yell while you hit with the pillow. Be careful not to hurt yourself. When you put your aggressive energy toward this action, you will release your emotion and the anger will decrease.

Underneath anger is often one of two emotions: sadness or fear. Once you start implementing these techniques, you may find that you gain insight into what is really bothering you. You may begin to cry or feel sad. If it is fear that lies underneath your anger, ask yourself what you are afraid of. I suggest writing your thoughts down in your notebook after trying this technique.

For more information on releasing emotions, check out **Tip#52: Releasing Bodily-Felt Emotions.**

Mindfulness in the Moment
Body Scanning Technique

People who are depressed and anxious tend to leave the moment, and their minds disconnect from their bodies. Your mind travels to what happened at work or an argument with your spouse. Your sadness or stress is focused on another point in time, which, past or present, *you do not have control over*.

I would like you to practice being present in your body, using this Body Scanning Technique. This exercise reconnects your mind to your body. If your thoughts are focused on your body, they cannot be lost in the past or future.

Try This!

Lie down flat on the floor, yoga mat, sofa or bed. Close your eyes and focus your mind on the toes of your left foot. Stay here for at least one minute. Notice the sensations in your toes. Allow your mind to slowly travel up the foot, lower leg, knee, thigh, and then to the pelvis. Next, focus on the toes of your right foot, then up the foot, lower leg, knee, thigh, and pelvis. Take a breath or two each time you focus on a new part of your body. As you exhale, let go of the tension you feel in that zone. With each breath in, imagine restorative and healing energy replacing the stress that once existed there. You may even want to visualize a calming color entering that area of your body.

Gradually move your mind's eye to your lower abdomen and lower back, the belly, next to the chest and shoulder blades, and then the shoulders. Then feel the sensation of your fingers on both hands, and let your mind wander up both arms simultaneously, returning to your shoulders. Don't forget to breathe in and out with each region of the body. Feel the roundness of your shoulders and their connection to your neck. Feel the throat and chin, lips, cheeks, nose, eyes, and eyebrows. Focus on the back of and, finally, the top of your head. Rest your focus there and imagine your breathing in a fluid motion throughout your body. Breathe in to the top of your body and exhale toward your toes, imagining your breathing as a slow wave upon a shore.

When this body scan is complete, you will feel the solidity of your entire body and, at the same time, feel as though your body is light and full of your breath. Each part of your body will vibrate with interconnectivity. Your mind will feel grounded to the whole body, and your anxiety will be far away.

Notice how your body feels in this moment. If you are noticing the calm and peace of right now, you will realize that there is nothing wrong within this time and space. Your anxiety comes from yesterday and worries of later today and tomorrow. If you can practice this technique and begin to own precious moments each day, you will create distance from your troubles.

Visualization Technique

To reach a goal, it is helpful to visualize what it will be like when you accomplish it. If you want to lose weight, you have to work with the goal of your ideal health and weight in mind. If you want to overcome depression, imagine yourself as a happy, positive, confident person—actually see this, vividly, in your mind.

The brain does not know the difference between imagination and reality. You can physically see this book you are holding and view it with your eyes. But then you can close your eyes and think of the same image, and your brain will not know the difference. We tend to think in pictures, and people who are depressed are always thinking negatively, and catastrophizing, even if their thoughts do not match reality. We worry about our future and visualize the worst-case scenarios. We visualize nothing but sadness, isolation, others leaving us, poor performance at work, and a bleak future. It's like we are watching a movie of all the things that can go wrong. This just creates more depression.

Try This!

Imagine how you will feel when you overcome depression. Imagine a successful, positive, happy you. Maybe imagine a time in the past where you felt and looked amazing. What would this life look like? What would it feel like? Feel the emotions as if you have already beat depression. When you imagine this new reality, your brain starts to believe that it is true! You release hormones that promote happiness and a feeling of calm. You teach yourself that this future is a possibility because you can feel it. You know what you are working toward when you are able to imagine it in detail.

Do this visualization every day, preferably in the morning. You are much more likely to get to this place if you can already see it in your mind.

Tapping to Calm You
Emotional Freedom Technique

Emotional Freedom Technique, or EFT, is a therapeutic technique that combines acupressure and affirmation to help you to overcome a particular issue. The process connects your body and your mind to fight against negative beliefs you may hold about yourself and your abilities. By repeating positive affirmations and using acupressure, you begin to feel the positive emotions throughout your body. This process will not miraculously cure your symptoms, but it will promote a sense of healing, self-love, and acceptance. These attributes are necessary in combating depression.

The Affirmation

The EFT affirmation is:

Even though I _____, I deeply and completely love and accept myself.

It is your role to think about which issue is really troubling you and holding you back. Then, complete the affirmation.

Some examples of this could be:

Even though I am angry, I deeply and completely love and accept myself.

Even though I have this fear of rejection, I deeply and completely love and accept myself.

Even though I am sad and depressed, I deeply and completely love and accept myself.

Even though I feel regret (e.g. over my recent actions at home), I deeply and completely love and accept myself.

Try This!

You will be using your fingertips to lightly tap specific acupressure points in your body known as meridians. Traditionally, the fingertips on your index and middle finger are used. Only one hand is used at a time. Begin at the top of your head, and work your way down through the meridians. You will tap each meridian 5–7 times, or about the length of a full, deep breath. As you gently tap these points on your body, you will be focusing on a specific issue you are facing. Repeat your affirmation at each point.

The Meridians

Top of the Head: Tap in the center, top portion of your head.

Eyebrow: Focus the tapping above the nose, where your eyebrow begins.

Side of the Eye: Tap on the bone next to the outside of your eye.

Under the Eye: Tap the bone under your pupil.

Under the Nose: Tap the small space between your nose and your upper lip.

Chin: Tap halfway between the point of your chin and the bottom of your lower lip.

Collar Bone: This point is actually 1 inch below your collar bone. To find this point, place your index finger on the notch at the bottom of your neck (where the knot rests in a tie), and next, move your finger 1 inch down, and one inch over to either side.

Under the Arm: On the side of the body, approximately 4 inches below the armpit.

Wrists: The last point is the inside of both wrists.

Meditation for Depression

Meditation is the focusing of one's breathing and thoughts in a quiet way to expand self-awareness and consciousness. Research has proved that this practice can foster feelings of calmness and self-compassion, enhance the body's immune functioning, and also reduce stress, anxiety, sadness, and pain.[1] The skills derived from meditation training have been shown to be effective in significantly reducing the recurrence of major depressive episodes by half in patients treated for depression.[2]

Try This!

I chose to share a breathing meditation here with you, though there are many kinds of meditation.

So how do you meditate? Well, it is a simple yet complicated process. Generally, you must find a quiet place for your meditation practice. It is recommended that you meditate daily in the same quiet space. You may sit in a traditional cross-legged position or any other seated position that is comfortable. You should try to maintain a straightened and aligned back.

The difficult part of getting started is quieting your thoughts. It can be a challenge to tune out your worries and troubles; and this is why focusing on one object, thought, or your breathing is helpful in meditation. Breathe naturally without trying to force or regulate your breath. Focus on the sensation of the air flowing in and out of your body.

At this point, you may be tempted to let your anxious or depressive thoughts take you away from the moment, but resist them and maintain focus on your breath. It is natural to become distracted at first. Just like training a dog to sit, you can train your mind to be still and to focus. Draw your attention to your breath, feeling the warm sensation as you inhale and exhale. Keep this focus for ten to fifteen minutes each day. If you find the length of time becomes a distraction, start with five minutes until you are comfortable and work your way up to an absolute minimum of 10 minutes per day. You should begin to notice a calm and *spacious* feeling in your mind and body. This spaciousness refers to the feeling of pain and worry settling, leaving room for calmness and compassion.

Those who practice meditation regularly rely on it to promote a sense of natural contentment and to keep stress at a minimum, allowing a sense of calm in all areas of life.

3 Tips to Get You Motivated

"Faith is taking the first step even when you don't see the whole staircase."
                              —Martin Luther King, Jr.

Behavioral Activation

Behavioral activation is a therapeutic technique that stimulates motivation by way of action. Action is the first step, and motivation follows.

Depressed individuals can become lethargic, fatigued, and apathetic. They lack interest and motivation to do the things they once enjoyed. They wait and wait for the motivation to do that task—to go to the store, to socialize, or to clean up—*but that feeling never comes.* The longer they lack motivation, the more difficult it is to stir up the energy inside of them to *just do something.*

Behavioral activation is basically a way to jump-start motivation. Rather than waiting for the feeling, just push yourself to take a step forward—to brush your teeth, make a meal, or spend time with a friend. When you actually do something, your sense of motivation will appear. *By acting, you create the feeling of motivation.* Eventually, your level of motivation will increase so that you are no longer forcing yourself to act.

Once you start participating in activities, getting outside, and talking to people, your mood will improve!

Try This!

Use the Activity Diary located in the appendix on page 126. Track your activity, rest, thoughts, and mood. You may notice that your mood spikes upward when you spend time with your family or when you get out of the house, as your mood tends to increase when you engage in activity, rather than being sedentary. The activity diary will allow you to see patterns in your mood and notice the peaks and valleys throughout the day. With this information, you will become aware of the activities you do and how they impact your mood. In turn, you will have more control over how you feel throughout the day.

Bring the Outside In![3]

Studies have shown that by simply recalling the memory of lush green surroundings, a city park, or the view from the top of a hike when you are experiencing times of stress or sadness can actually lighten your mood. Why do you think so many people have their computer background set to pictures of beaches, mountain tops, sunsets, or gardens? Not to make them bitter that they are stuck inside, but to *remind them of the exhilarating feeling of being surrounded by natural beauty.*

Try This!

First of all, everyone should have a plant in their office and/or home. Find a variety that is easy to care for and suits the size of your space.

Place around your office and home some visual reminders of vacations, hikes, or trips that you have taken. When experiencing a particularly stressful day, look at photos of the times you have spent in nature and recall the feeling that it gave you. Recalling your own memories of nature will instantly calm you down and increase your energy.

Visualize yourself surrounded by whatever nature scene makes you feel happy and peaceful. The simple act of **thinking about nature** can boost your energy almost as much as being there.

Get Outside[3]

Do you feel sluggish, exhausted, or bored? Recent findings published in the *Journal of Environmental Psychology* indicated that people who spent time in natural settings felt more alive, instantly had more energy, and had a heightened sense of well-being.

We often reach for caffeine when feeling fatigued, but this research suggests that simply placing ourselves in the outdoors for a brief period of time can instantly boost our mood and energy level. Just 20 minutes each day is enough to significantly boost vitality. Obviously being in the presence of nature is difficult for those who spend their days in office buildings, but there are ways to incorporate nature into your lifestyle.

Try This!

Instead of taking a coffee break, *take an outdoor break*. Eat your lunch outside; or if the weather does not permit it, sit in a sunlit corner of a coffee shop, concourse, or a part of your office other than your desk. Make sure that you can see the outside world, even if your view simply consists of buildings. Being in the sunlight releases Vitamin D in your body, boosting your mood and energy levels.

Managing Your Guilt

If you are constantly taking care of your partner, friends, children, or parents, you may be ignoring your own needs. You feel guilty when you say no to others. You silence your opinion because it is easier than having an argument. You give up the things you want because you don't want to fight for them. You may worry about what others may think of you if you decided to speak up. You continue to deny your feelings.

When you silence yourself, you are turning your emotions inward and allowing depression to build. Silencing the self can also mean that you are not taking care of yourself, which can lead to physical illness, muscle tension, fatigue, anxiety, and depression.

I want you to *imagine yourself* as an assertive person. This is what it would look and feel like:

> *You value your needs and opinions.*
> *You have time to do the things you want and need to do because you have set boundaries with others.*
> *You are not hiding in silence and self-doubt, but you are expressing yourself with confidence.*
> *You don't allow resentment for others to build because you are expressing yourself in your relationships.*
> *You are saying no. You will not allow yourself to be taken advantage of.*

Try This!

Attempt to sit with the guilt that you feel after you say no to someone. *We often say yes, instead of no, because if it is too difficult to be with the guilt.* I encourage you to sit with it, with a notebook in hand, and write out your feelings and thoughts. If you sit with the guilt, *it will pass.* But by avoiding it, saying yes, and putting yourself last, you will only build resentment because you are, yet again, doing something that you do not want to do.

Use "I" statements to express how you feel about a situation or circumstance. For example, "I don't feel heard when I tell you that I am not able to do that."

Tip #11

Practice Being Assertive

Be sure to read **Tip #10** before trying this tip.

Try This!

When attempting to be assertive, try not to become defensive or manipulative. When faced with a problem, confront it.

Change your body language: use direct eye contact and engage your body (lean forward with interest, do not cross your arms or lean back). Keep your voice confident and even and avoid emotional wavering. Try breathing deep into your belly.

Practice being assertive with people that you don't know very well. Say "No, thank you," politely and repeatedly. Do not make excuses and be firm.

Being assertive does not mean that you are selfish; it means that you respect and value yourself. Many depressed individuals have lost these qualities after so much time spent denying their emotions. I encourage you to think about how good it would feel to stand up for your beliefs and to express your feelings. You will feel relief if you take even a

few steps towards assertiveness. Soon it will become a habit, and people will start to relate to you differently. In order to be a good wife, mother, friend, father, husband, or child, or whatever role you fill, you must first "fill yourself" up, or you will have nothing left to give others. Self-care and self-compassion are healthy and necessary.

Remember: When you say yes to someone when you want to say no, you are saying no to yourself.

Tip #12

Increasing Social Connection

Depression tends to cause social withdrawal and a lack of connection with others. You may feel too tired, overwhelmed, or sad to talk to anyone. You may avoid phone calls and social events, whereas you used to have great relationships with friends and family. When you are disconnected from others for a while, it begins to contribute to your negativity. When you are isolated, you are alone with your sabotaging thoughts, and it becomes easier for depression to take over. Become aware of your level of isolation. When was the last time you talked to a friend on the phone? When was the last time you went out with a friend or attended a party or dinner?

If you were to connect with the friend or family member you selected earlier in this book, you could get support and encouragement, share a laugh, recall great memories, and participate in activities. This acts as a distraction and a release from your inner turmoil. Remember that sometimes our negative thoughts get in the way of moving forward and being social even though we want to. You may have the *intention to act* but have difficulty acting. This is normal when you are depressed. For information on how to overcome your negative thoughts and get into action, flip to **Tip #15: Listen To Your Positive Voice.** For tips on how to get motivated, flip to **Tip #7: Behavioral Activation.**

If you really feel overwhelmed by going out of your house, at least try to connect socially on the phone or the internet. You can even join a forum online to connect with others who have shared interests without the anxiety of meeting new people. Immerse yourself in a discussion and really engage with others. Remember that in this book, there are techniques to help you overcome the anxiety of meeting new people and putting yourself out there. If you feel anxious in social situations, practice **Tip#1: Diaphragmatic Breathing.** This form of breathing will help calm you.

The more you spend time with others, the easier it will be to make socializing a habit. Your mood will improve as you increase your connections, rather than being stuck in your own thoughts.

Try This!

Call, text, or email a friend right now to make a plan to get together. You don't have to go out right now, but set a date and time. Let your friend know that you are feeling down, and ask him or her to hold you accountable to get together more often. Ask your friend to not allow you to cancel. At first, try going out just once each week and meet someone for coffee.

If you don't have a friend or family member close by, look up a group that you can join online. However you connect with others, try to start the process immediately after reading this tip.

To connect with individuals who are also going through similar issues, I recommend visiting an online forum like www.depressionforums.org. Remember, you are not alone.

Tips to Shift Your Negative Thinking

"*People suffer because they are caught in their views. As soon as we release those views, we are free and we don't suffer anymore.*"

—Thich Nhat Hanh

Tip #13

Smile Exercise

The emotional part of your brain sends signals to your facial muscles so that your expression can reflect the way you feel. This process can also work in another way, so that the expression on your face stimulates an emotional response in your brain. Try crossing your brow and glaring ... didn't you feel angry for just that second? Depression in the mind reflects facial expressions of sadness—or most often, a blank or apathetic look. Even if you are not feeling happy in this moment, generating a smile on your face will cause a happier emotional response in the brain.

Try It!

I urge you to take a few minutes now and sit quietly with your eyes closed. Relax and form a half-smile on your face. You don't have to grin wildly and force the smile; simply turn up the corners of your mouth. Feel that smile as it radiates through your face. Drop your shoulders and imagine the effects of the smile traveling through your mind and body. Feel that smile as a sort of calm heat and focus the warm energy on the parts of your body that might be feeling pain or stress.

As you breathe in, think of the word "calm." As you breathe out, think of the word "joy" and ensure that your mouth is continually, yet softly, smiling. Allow yourself to feel calm, serene, and peaceful. Focus on your smile and the feelings it gives you and try to keep the mind quiet. Practice this tip often and try to carry the half-smile with you throughout your day.

A smile is like a small dose of happiness for your brain, and it creates an inner calm and contentment. A smile is also contagious; and if you are reflecting positivity toward others, they will reciprocate.

"A smile is the beginning of peace."
                                        –Mother Teresa

Rubber Band Technique

Try This!

Wear a rubber band around your wrist and snap it whenever you catch yourself having a negative thought. This process literally "snaps" you back into reality. You will never be able to stop your negative thoughts completely, as they are a part of you; however, you can become more aware of them and their destructive nature.

Snapping the rubber band allows you to draw attention to and respond to the negativity, instead of allowing the negative inner chatter to consume you and stop you. Next time you think that you can't do something, snap out of it!

Listen to Your Positive Voice

Each one of us is made up of many parts. We have the critical part, the anxious part, the guilt-ridden part, and many more! However, we also have positive and encouraging parts of us—the parts that tell us to say no or to treat ourselves. Clients often ask me how to get rid of the negative voice in their heads. This is the voice that tells you that something is inherently wrong with you, that something bad is going to happen, that it's not going to work out, etc. However, many of us are so used to listening to the critical side of ourselves that the positive side has been almost completely drowned out.

Once you become aware of this negative inner chatter, you can gain control of it and learn to focus on your positive and uplifting thoughts instead.

You can learn to become aware of the critical part of you; and *through awareness, you can gain control*. You can learn to reframe your sabotaging inner chatter into an encouraging inner voice.

Visualize this scenario right now: Picture yourself driving a car. You can turn left or right, and you can make this life choice or that life choice. There are two people in the back seat, each trying to tell you where to go. One of them is the positive, encouraging voice who is caring toward the self. The other person is the critical part of yourself who is shouting out negative comments, fighting to be louder than the positive part. As the driver in the car (and the person in charge of your own life), *it is up to you to learn which part of yourself to listen to*. If you pay attention to the critical part of

yourself, you will always hear negative chatter that gives you the wrong directions, tells you that you aren't good enough, or tells you that you can't accomplish your goals. If you were really in a car with this type of negative and hurtful person, you would probably turn around and tell them to shut up! That's the exact type of courage you need to quiet that negative voice in your head.

It's about learning to disregard the critical voice and paying attention to the other one—the encouraging one. This takes practice. It's like working a muscle: the more you exercise it, the easier it becomes. The more you tell that negative voice that it's wrong, the easier it will become to listen to the positive. *You will begin to feel those positive thoughts as true, and you will no longer be distracted by discouraging thoughts and fears.*

Try This!

The next time you are feeling down, I'd like you to stop and notice the inner chatter that you are listening to. Then, pretend that it's a good friend saying those negative things about himself or herself. What encouraging words would you say to cheer that friend up? Say these things to yourself and notice how different you feel. Write about this negative voice in your journal and jot down the soothing words you have told yourself.

Distract Yourself

Maybe you don't have the energy to practice a therapeutic technique or talk about how you feel. You might be caught in a whirlwind of sadness, lethargy, and depression. If this is the case, think about what action you can do right now to shift your mood. What can you do to literally distract yourself from your negative thoughts? Although this is not a cure for depression overall, it is a method to ease the sadness you are feeling in the moment.

This is a tip about changing your behavior in the moment. Keep this in mind next time you are feeling particularly low.

Try This!

Play a video game, read a book, watch television, cook a meal, or play with your pet. Call someone who makes you laugh. Distract yourself with work, or check your email. *Change your behavior in the moment. Do something that you are interested in enough that it will take your focus away from your negative, self-defeating thoughts.* Do something that is a completely different behavior.

Keep in mind that this is a temporary escape from your sadness. Changing your behavior in the moment may seem like denying your feelings; however, sometimes your thoughts are harming you, and you may benefit from a distraction to help stop the negative self-talk. There are times when you need to ignore your thoughts and do something else before your negative thoughts engulf you and ruin your day.

If you are doing something you like to do, it is more difficult to focus on your sadness.

Opposite of Emotion Technique

This is an exercise in which you *replace* the negative feelings you are having with more positive feelings. *Try to behave in a way that is opposite to the way you are feeling.* By doing so, you are able to decrease the negativity and feel more calm and happy in the moment. A negative feeling could include anger, nervousness, or sadness.

In some cases, this technique is about replacing inaction with action. For example, if you feel lethargic or unmotivated, you must push yourself to become active or find the motivation you are missing. Do something that you are good at or enjoy. Participate in an activity that makes you feel confident and capable.

If you are experiencing feelings of anger, use the energy that is feeding your anger toward doing something nice. For example, if you are upset at someone, imagine how you might be empathetic toward them, rather than placing blame. Take it a step further and do something nice for that person.

This technique may also seem as though you are denying your feelings. However, when you are stuck in a depressed mindset, your negative thoughts can actually intensify the emotions you are feeling. The anger or sadness could be a result of your frustration or feelings of helplessness. By acting in a way that is opposite from your emotions, you can reduce the negative feelings you have.

Tip #17

Try This!

List the actual negative emotions you experienced today and identify those positive feelings or actions you used to overcome them. The key is that when you are feeling anger or sadness, for example, focus that energy on the opposite emotion. Document both later in your notebook.

Turn these issues:	Into something new:
Anger	Acceptance, Love, Generosity
Sadness	Positivity
Inactivity	Activity
Isolation	Social Connection
Blame	Understanding

A Single Minute Exercise

Just like most of us, you probably do not perceive time accurately. This simple exercise can help you gain a better sense of the present moment. Present moment awareness is often helpful for those experiencing depression, as it promotes a feeling of calm and a sort of attentiveness toward the body, rather than the mind. For example, we often rush through our day feeling as though we have too many things to do and not enough time to accomplish it all. When you keep your focus on the next thing you have to do, you lose sight of the present. However, the present is the only moment we can truly experience, despite the fact that most of us worry about the future.

Try This!

To complete this brief exercise, find a quiet place to sit or lay down, away from others. Time yourself with a stopwatch, or look at the clock as you begin. Now, stay still in your comfortable position with your eyes closed or open, breathing deeply. Resist the urge to count the seconds; and when you think that one minute has passed, stop the timer or look again at the clock. *Notice how much time has actually passed.* Either way, an incorrect assessment indicates that you can benefit from focusing on the present.

What were your results?

If you stopped the clock at well under a minute, do you tend to have a sense of urgency in your life, like you're not doing enough? You will notice when doing this exercise that one minute can feel like a long time when you are *still and present*. Sometimes, by slowing down, you will actually feel *less overwhelmed*.

Did you stop at well past a minute? If so, do you tend to procrastinate? Do you often think, "Well, I'll just do it later because I'll have time then"? This can often lead to a sense of feeling overwhelmed if you must scramble to complete tasks at the last moment. From time to time, calmly consider what can be accomplished in the present.

Reframe Your Depressed Thinking

We often react to internal beliefs we hold that are not actually rooted in reality. For example, we become anxious when someone is rude or short with us, and we may assume it is our fault. Or if running late for work, we may worry that it will lead to disciplinary measures or being fired. Once stuck in the spiral of anxiety, the body may react in ways such as muscle tension, headaches, racing heart, and shortness of breath. Cognitive Behavioral Therapy provides a technique for coping with our irrational internal beliefs. This technique is called Cognitive Reframing. You can utilize this same technique in the exercise below.

Try This!

When we are feeling down, it is usually because our thoughts are dictating how we feel, and they often lead to stress. The next time you feel down, ask yourself, "What was I thinking?" Irrational thoughts can be on any issue. The example below is only to guide you through this process.

My friend must be mad at me because she didn't call me back.

Ask yourself . . .
1. Is there any other way to look at this?
2. Is this thought realistic?
3. Is there any other way I could think about this?
   Is there anything in this moment that I can do?

4. In the grand scheme of things, is this really that bad?

Next, tell a new story to yourself that is opposite from your former perception.

My friend might be busy or upset; so to be a good friend, I will let her know that I am there for her if she needs to talk. I am not going to take it personally—maybe it has nothing to do with me. Even if my friend is upset with me, I am sure we will work it out. Everything will be ok. I have had friends mad at me in the past, and everything turned out all right. I am a strong person and have overcome a lot. Even though this may be stressful, I know I will get through this.

Examine the thought and change it by REFRAMING it. After a while, our negative thoughts build up and can become beliefs we hold about ourselves. This technique is about looking at the thought through a more realistic and positive view instead of an irrational and negative view. *Reframing allows us to consciously tell ourselves a different story; and by doing so, we can form new beliefs.*

In your notebook, examine a thought that is causing you stress. Go through the list above to reframe this thought, and notice how you feel afterward. Remember that anytime you feel down, you can try this exercise. You can change how you feel in the moment just by reframing your thoughts.

Challenging Your Beliefs

Just as a therapist would work with you to understand the root of your behavior, your innermost thoughts, you can do so much on your own. What are the thoughts that lead to your actions? Why do you think the way you do? Once you change your thoughts, your behaviors will change, and *you will start to feel better*. Perhaps you can dispel one negative thought today by completing the following exercise.

Try This!

A popular technique used in therapy is one in which the therapist helps to identify and then challenge your existing thought patterns. This is done in a questioning process that can prove to be very insightful. You can practice this yourself; and in doing so, you may discover that your existing feelings about yourself have no supporting evidence. The questions and responses provided are only examples to illustrate. Maybe your belief is different. For example: "*I fail at everything.*" The point is to select a negative belief that is impacting or controlling your life and follow this same exercise. If it helps, write down your questions and answers in your notebook. <u>Take a current belief that you have.</u> For example, *"There is no point in trying to overcome my depression because it will just come back again."*

Ask yourself the following questions:

Is there any *evidence* (actual facts) for this belief?
(Sample responses only. How would you respond?)

"Yes, I was depressed five years ago, and it did come back because I am depressed again."

What is the *evidence against* this belief? *This is key because we usually don't think about evidence that does not support our beliefs; we focus on the times when our beliefs were proven.

"Yes, I went through long periods of not being depressed; and the last time I was depressed, I bounced back much faster."

"I have had friends who were severely depressed in the past and it has not come back. I see them using certain tools to feel better when they do feel down."

What is the worst that can happen if you give up this belief? *"I can only think of good things happening if I let go of this belief."*

What is the best that can happen if you give up this belief? *"I will trust myself and have hope about the future, which would make me feel relieved and happy."*

When you think about the best thing that could happen if you were able to let go of your negative beliefs, it should motivate you to replace those negative thoughts with positive, or at least neutral, thoughts.

Name Your Negative Voice

We all have a voice inside that makes us doubt our dreams and our goals. This voice might tell you that you aren't good enough, that you will fail and people will judge you, or that the things you hope for in life are out of your reach. While the voice might always be there, **you can learn to tune it out**.

Try This!

Take a moment and think about how your thoughts can change and don't have to control your reality. **Become aware of the fact that you have been stuck with a routine thought, but it is not reflective of the true you.** You can be going about your day when the negativity creeps in and ruins it. Try to catch the moment where your day turns from all right to hopeless. **Give your negative voice a name;** and as soon as it appears, tell it to go away. Some of us have a Sergeant that lives in our head telling us to push harder and that what we are doing isn't enough. You may want to visualize that voice as another person, separate from yourself. Or you may have a Worrier or a Critic that lives in your head—or all three! Visualize him or her in front of you. If you could visualize this voice, personified, what would this Critic look like? Then give this person a name. Act as if it is another person, separate from your own identity, who is too negative to be around. Push that critic away in your mind and imagine yourself being completely protected from that "other" person's negativity. This will assist you in not getting tangled up in your negative thoughts. You will continue to hear the voices (your thoughts); but you can get to the point where you are able to disregard the negative thoughts, choosing to ignore the Worrier's, the Sergeant's, or the Critic's voice. You know that it's just negative chatter, and it's not real. You stop listening to the sabotaging thoughts.

Shift Your Focus

Today, I want you to think about where your focus lies. Think about what and who most of your thoughts and feelings are directed at.

If you are in a depressed state, you will have the tendency to be self-focused. This is very common. You may think about yourself and your situation in a negative light. You may focus on regrets (the past) or worry (the future). After a while, your view will continue to narrow until there is no room for anyone else.

Try This!

Imagine your focus is a camera. The lens you are using is a negative, distorted lens. It focuses on you, your needs, your thoughts, and your feelings. Once each day, I want you to imagine that you are replacing this lens with a new one, even if it is just for a few minutes. Imagine that this new lens is positive and focused on others in your life. It's all right to think about your life; however, you want to focus on your life in relation to others.

Who are you grateful for in your life? Who is special to you? What could you do for someone else that would make that person feel great?

Focusing on someone else, for even a short time, allows an escape from a self-focused, depressed viewpoint. Doing this regularly helps to heal a sense of isolation and breaks the pattern of negative, inwardly focused thoughts.

Thought Stopping Techniques

Depression often goes hand in hand with anxiety. Sadness and worry can also be very closely connected. Next time you have an anxious or worrisome thought, try these "Thought Stopping" techniques.

Try This!

- Picture a stop sign popping up directly in front of you, blocking you from your negative thoughts.
- Imagine your worry in a balloon and visualize yourself letting it go. See it travel up into the sky and watch it disappear.
- Replace your thought with a completely opposite, positive thought. For example, if you constantly worry about your unknown future, try thinking about what you are grateful for in the present.
- Name your negative voice. Treat that negative voice as a separate identity that exists outside of yourself. Each time you hear a negative thought, tell that person to shut up! By thinking of that voice as someone you don't like—someone who does not support you and lacks the confidence you have—it becomes easier to quiet the voice.

Most importantly, track the negativity. When does the negativity come up? What seems to prompt the negative feelings? Becoming aware of the negativity is the first step toward blocking it out.

5 Tips to Overcome Your Fear

"*Breathe in trust, breathe out fear.*"

Exposure Therapy Journaling

Feeling and Letting Go of Trauma

Depression is often related to the past and a trauma, or multiple traumas that occurred. The memory of these incidents can block you from moving forward and from finding happiness. The incident may linger in your mind and create an ongoing sense of fear, mistrust, or sadness. When we experience a trauma, we tend to avoid these memories and push them down because they are too painful. However, they create an emotional charge that can run your life, so it is best to bring them out into the light and overcome them.

Journaling about a traumatic event, an event we most likely have tried hard to *not* think about, causes the event to lose its emotional charge. We will always remember that it happened, but it will no longer have a hold on us emotionally. Writing our story about this unpleasant, scary experience, can be an effective type of exposure therapy. When we face the incident that we have been pushing down for so long, we can finally move on.

If you have a strong social network, you may rely on the support of friends and family after completing this exercise. If the memories prove to be too painful or emotional, be sure to contact your support person.

Try This!

Grab your journal and pen. You also want to make sure you put your journal in a place where you are fairly certain others will not find it—this way, you can freely vent your deepest emotions and thoughts.

Once you are in a comfortable place, start writing! Write the event down—*over and over again*. Retell the incident until a complete and vivid picture of the event comes to mind. You may need to write the event ten times! Keep writing about it, as many times as you need to, until it loses its emotional charge—until your emotional reaction is less intense. This can bring up flashbacks and nightmares. It can be traumatic to relive the experience at first, but the nervous system adjusts as you continually retell the event. The anxiety and fear also decreases. The trauma becomes less and less intense, and you will be able to gain emotional distance from it. The more this technique is practiced, the more acclimated you will become toward the trauma. It will feel unpleasant, but the emotions and sensations in your body should be tolerable. You are taking the steps to move on. If your emotions become intolerable contact your support person.

Letting Go of Guilt

Guilt can invade your thoughts and take over. You may have thoughts such as: "I feel bad, I feel guilty, I feel that I could do more, I feel responsible, I shouldn't have done that, I should have said yes."

When I meet with a client who is experiencing a lot of guilt, I ask about their childhood. There is usually a connection in the child/parent relationship that has led to guilty feelings in adulthood. For example, it is often the case that this individual's parents were overly critical. In turn, the child became self-critical. Guilt leads to perfectionistic tendencies in adulthood and a need to be in control.

Guilt is a heavy, hard emotion to live with. Since it is difficult to handle, we often distract ourselves by doing things that ease our guilt. We care for others. We say yes when we mean no. We spend more time thinking about and nurturing others' needs than our own. We take over tasks due to our need to be in control. A client once told me, "I can't say no to my mom because I'll feel guilty, so instead I just do what she asks." As a result of making this choice, my client becomes resentful towards herself and her mom for saying yes when she means no.

A feeling of guilt means that we are feeling responsible for someone or something else. It is important to know that you are responsible for your *own* happiness more so than the happiness of others. You are not really caring for or taking care of others if you are robbing yourself of your own well-being.

Try This!

A good way to overcome any negative emotion is to be still and feel the emotion. Rather than care taking, do the opposite and literally sit and feel your guilt. **If you sit with it, it will eventually go away.** It won't necessarily feel good while you sit with it; but if you don't just feel the feeling, the guilt will continue to run your choices, and you will continue to be tired and an angry giver.

The next time you have the impulse to say yes, try saying what you really want to say, which may be no. Then sit, be still, and feel your emotions. You may cry, and you may feel angry. If this happens, I suggest writing in your notebook or calling a supportive friend.

Tip #26 ✓

Let Go and Cry

A common symptom of depression is holding back tears. Many people experiencing depression have a difficult time crying. A lot of my clients fear that if they start crying, they won't be able to stop. So instead of crying, they bottle up their emotions, leaving no outlet.

However, another symptom of depression is uncontrollable crying. Maybe you are tearful at work, even at inappropriate times. Your emotions spill over and interfere with your daily life. In this case, examine your thoughts. Where does your focus lie? See **Tip #30: Feel Better with Focus,** and answer those questions to really understand where your thoughts are leading you.

Crying accompanies many emotions: anger, nervousness, happiness, and sadness. It is the physical release and healing of an emotional problem. The body wants to have a release; but more often than not, we hold back. Crying can sometimes be seen as a weakness or a sign of a lack of control, yet we shouldn't have to fight the urge to cry. It should be as socially acceptable as laughing or smiling. It is simply another way that the human body expresses emotion.

When we feel anxious or stressed, we often experience tenseness in our chest and knots in our throat or stomach. This bodily tension can often be released when we allow ourselves to let go and cry. I encourage you to allow yourself to cry on a weekly basis. I know it seems like a lot, but it will help you sleep and help you release tension and pain from your body. Have faith that you will stop crying when you are finished releasing the emotion. Your first cry might be longer, as you have likely kept your emotions inside for so long. With practice, brief bouts of crying will make you feel better almost instantly. In the case of crying too much, practice the same advice I have recommended to those who cannot cry. Set aside an appropriate time and place to release your emotions. If you slow down, listen to your body, and release your emotions, your tears won't surprise you and interfere with your day.

Try This!

Some people don't even know how to start crying. Here is how to have a good cry:

When you are alone, perhaps before bed, practice breathing deeply. Focus your breathing toward your heart. Be patient and just spend some time in your body, focusing on the inhale and exhale of your breath. Breathe in and out from the heart. Relax and let the stress, frustration, and any other emotions you are feeling flood out of you in the form of tears. Imagine that, as you cry, these emotions are released from your body and you are free of them.

Try it tonight if you can. You will notice a relief right away. Be patient; if you have difficulty being emotional, it may take some time for you to let go. Just try your best to quiet your thoughts by breathing and relaxing your body, focus on your heart, breathe through the physical tension you are feeling in your body, and let it come! Crying is healthy, and it's needed. What a wonderful ability we have!

Tips to Give You Insight

"At any given moment you have the power to say: This is not how the story is going to end."

—Christine Mason Miller

Non-Dominant Handwriting Technique

We all have fears, hopes, and emotions that we keep tucked away deep inside ourselves. It can be difficult to answer what may seem like simple questions such as, "What is blocking me? Why do I continually self-sabotage?" When we are children and adolescents, we rely on our emotions and intuitions to guide us; but as we mature, we start to focus on the rational side of the self. Yet our emotions can help us uncover our own roadblocks, and our intuition will guide us toward the things we want. I encourage you to try this technique—to discover your internal, guiding compass.

Try This!

First, write down the following list of questions in your notebook using your dominant hand. (If you are right-handed, it would be your right hand). Leave a space below each question as you will fill in the answers afterward.

- Why am I sad?
- What is blocking me?
- What do I need to let go of?
- Who do I need to forgive?
- What payoff am I getting from my behavior?

Next, to answer the questions, switch the pen or pencil to your non-dominant hand. The use of your other hand allows your ever-present conscious mind to be still. Research shows that most of our choices and actions are run by our subconscious. There is a lot of wisdom locked in your subconscious mind that is directing your choices, even though you are not aware of your internal motivators. This exercise will allow you to access and become aware of why you sabotage yourself. With that awareness, you can start making different choices.

End of Day Reflection

It is important to evaluate your life and your happiness frequently. We can all become so busy that we often forget to check in with ourselves. When our lives are taken over by work, family, and stress, our physical and mental health often move to the bottom of the priority list.

Try This!

Check in with yourself tonight before bed, and continue this nightly over the next week. Repeat the process as needed. Focus and reflect on what went right today and where things went wrong. Real change can only be made if you take the time to notice your patterns, your triggers, and your negative thoughts. What, or who, impacted your day to turn badly? Why did this happen? We all have triggers; and when you think back over the last few days, something most likely caused you to feel angry, upset, hurt, or anxious. *When we experience these negative emotions, we have to pause and take a moment to reflect on where they are coming from.* It is usually about a much larger issue, not just about your partner doing something to upset you or a co-worker being late for a meeting.

When we spend our lives on autopilot, we keep making the same mistakes and getting in the same arguments. Notice the negative thoughts and emotions you had today and in the last few days. Ask yourself what those feelings reminded you of. Was there another time in your life when you felt like that?

When you notice that the negativity stems from a pattern and not a particular event, it is easier to let it go in the moment. For example, maybe your boss is micro-managing you and you become agitated. But then you think ... *"Wait a second; this is how I felt when my dad was always critical of me when I was a kid.—not good enough, frustrated, and angry ..."* In that moment, you realize that you are so upset because you feel not good enough in some way. While your boss is wrong in doing that, he is not the same person your anger was directed toward in the past. Instead of unleashing those built-up feelings, become aware that you have been triggered. In doing this, you are much more likely to take a deep breath and let it go, and your emotional reaction will pass. When we take time to examine the source of our emotions, we are less likely to have such intense reactions. *You are not the same person you used to be. You can choose to be happy and positive, right now, in this moment.*

So take time at the end of each day to reflect, let go, and move forward. It would be helpful to write some of your experiences in your notebook as an additional aid to letting go.

Empty Chair & Expressive Writing Technique

The Empty Chair Technique allows a person to uncover an aspect of a conflict they are struggling with. It can allow insight and even resolution to an issue. A person will sit facing an empty chair and begin a "dialogue" with an imagined representation of another person or aspects of him or herself.

This technique allows a person to express emotion and move from a passive state, where they are thinking about a conflict, to an *immediate, experiential state*. In this exercise, the person is actively engaged in the issue at hand.

We are usually identified only with one side of a conflict. By getting in touch with both sides of an issue, we begin to understand it, and we become less consumed by it. The process stimulates an emotional response. It clarifies your feelings and can enlighten your understanding of that conflict. When we have insight toward both sides of a conflict, a solution may emerge naturally.

Despite the effectiveness of this technique, if you are looking to resolve a conflict with another person, you may need to seek additional help from a trained psychotherapist.

Try This!

You can use a similar technique at home to uncover two parts of your inner self. You may be torn about a certain aspect of your life, such as getting a divorce versus staying with your partner, or staying at your current job versus embarking on a new career path. Doing this at home does not require that you use different chairs or have the guidance of a therapist. A useful tool is to write from the perspectives of your conflicted parts.

Flip to an empty page in your notebook. On the top of the page, write what one part of you wants. On a separate page, write what the other part of you wants. Now you are allowing both parts of you to have a voice. In the first person, state how each part feels, what it needs, what it wants, and what it is afraid of. This will be a very insightful process allowing both aspects of yourself to be expressed, and you will leave this exercise with a sense of clarity. Certain feelings may come up that you were not aware of.

Feel Better with Focus

We are so used to negative thoughts that we often stop noticing them. Some negative thoughts include:

- *It's not going to work out.*

- *I'm not smart (or capable, independent, strong, or
  attractive).*

- *I'll never get ahead.*

- *I'll never meet someone.*

- *I have failed as a partner (or parent, friend, or
  employee).*

- *Something is wrong with me.*

Once we recognize where our focus lies, we can start
to change our thoughts, and in turn, our beliefs about ourselves. *Next time you catch yourself thinking negatively, try to
be as understanding of yourself as you would be to a friend.* If
your friend told you that they felt stupid or hopeless, you
would instantly point out their positive attributes and comfort them.

Try This!

When you lay in bed at night, and you are trying to fall asleep ... what thoughts are troubling you?

Pay attention to your internal mantra...what are you thinking?

Actually take a moment to write down your thoughts. You may be surprised at the negative conversation in your mind.

Show some compassion toward yourself. Comfort yourself and focus on your own positives. If you feel you have failed, create a plan to succeed next time. If you worry about perceived shortcomings, focus on ways to better yourself. Most of all, try to accept and let go of the past. Focus on a positive future.

Gratitude Exercise[4,5]
Why Be Grateful?

In his Gratitude Interventions Project, Dr. David Emmons of the University of California discovered several amazing components of living a grateful life. He and his team of researchers found that when you keep a weekly gratitude journal, you are more optimistic about life in general. In addition, the participants in the study exercised more regularly, reported fewer physical symptoms, and came closer to achieving their goals.

When a group of young adults began to practice daily gratitude interventions, they reported high levels of alertness, enthusiasm, determination, attentiveness, and energy compared to another group who focused on life's hassles and compared themselves to others. This group was also more likely to become helpful to others.

Practice being grateful. Actually thank those around you for making your life better. Make this a habit, and it will eventually feel natural. You will begin to notice that your life is full of blessings because you will be attracting positive energy.

Try This!

Write down ten things you are grateful for. Try this daily for 21 days. Even doing it once will make a difference in your outlook. It will get easier over the 21 days. Try to come up with different things each day, no matter how small they seem.

What's working in your life? What makes you smile? Who makes you happy? Who do you love? Who loves you? For some, this might take a while. If you struggle to come up with things you are grateful for, think of what others have said about you in the past. Has anyone ever thanked you for helping them? Perhaps you are generous or helpful. Try to feel gratitude about certain attributes you have, the people who are in your life, and the skills you have acquired. By focusing on the good, you will begin to feel good yourself.

Releasing Trauma

This is a self-directed exercise to explore, process, reflect, and let go of trauma. Depression happens because of a variety of factors, but it can often be attributed to a traumatic experience. This experience could have happened to you either a long time ago or even just recently. We hold this trauma inside our bodies, and it influences our behaviors and can cause us to become fearful. No two people are alike. You can experience the same trauma as someone else but react completely differently. *It is about what it means to you in your life today*.

Think about your wounds and traumatic experiences and journal in your notebook about what they mean to you now. If you are not exploring or reflecting on it, you cannot let it go.

Try This!

In your journal:

1. **Explore the trauma. What happened?**
   By writing down the details, you are able to process it in a different way.

2. **Why? Why do you think that this happened to you? What meaning does it hold for you now?**
   Let go. Imagine your life without this trauma and the fear holding you back. What could you be and achieve without it? Now visualize that the experience is gradually leaving your mind and body.

If thoughts of your past traumas continue to haunt you, keep doing this exercise. Don't shut out the experience, but reflect on the meaning it holds for you and start letting go.

When we reflect on what happened to us and notice what the experience has meant to us, we begin to understand how our past traumas shape our views of ourselves and the world. Digging deeper to examine these traumatic experiences often provides insight and healing.

Tip #33 ⬚⬚⬚⬚

What Is Depression Giving You?

Sometimes we hold onto things because they are working for us. This is a hard but good question: What is your depression giving you?

There are subconscious motivations that cause our actions and our moods. We are likely to repeat actions that make us feel good in some way. After experiencing persistent depression, on a subconscious level, it may be *easier to remain depressed because it's what we know.* It is somehow familiar. Overcoming this sadness may seem like too great of a battle.

Your depression may be giving you certain benefits that you crave such as the care, attention, and closeness with others that you desire. It might give you a reason to hide from the world. If you are lethargic and unmotivated, it could mean that others are taking care of you.

This is not to say that your depression is a conscious choice. However, in order to let go of your sadness, *you first have to let go of the part of your sadness that is serving you.*

Try This!

Think about what you might be gaining from your depression. Is there any benefit you are receiving from your depression? Write down the positive things you experience as a result:

The following are some examples, not necessarily what you are experiencing:

- Not working
- Family support
- Attention
- Care from others

Are you ready to let those things go and perhaps replace them with something new? Remember that you will still have the love and support of those around you once you are feeling good again. Once we let go of what is not serving us, we often make room for other new things to come into our life.

Inner Child Exercise

By the time you are 4 or 5, you have developed about 90% of the self-esteem and self-worth you will have for the rest of your life. If you felt unloved as a child—like a burden, neglected, not good enough, disappointed, or fearful—you could spend your whole life feeling that way. There is a sub-conscious part of you that holds all of the hurt, trauma, anger, and sadness of childhood. *The issues you face as an adult are often brought about by the child part of you that never healed.* Your inner child is calling out for attention, love, and healing. *Going back and healing the hurt is an important exercise. This allows you to move on and let go of the limiting beliefs that hold you back in life.*

Think of an issue that is blocking you from achieving something or being happy. Maybe it's an area of your life that you keep sabotaging. *The inner child is responsible for some of these patterns, and it is important to resolve these issues in order to find peace and achieve what you want in life.*

Try This!

In a relaxed state, with your eyes closed, see your 5-year-old self in front of you. See your child self in your imagination. Notice what you are wearing: the color of your clothing and even your haircut. Really ignite the image of your child self in your mind.

Now I would like you to bring up a particular memory, maybe even a painful memory—one that may have helped shape you into who you are today. Perhaps you felt helpless or afraid. Think about that

time and try to really feel it in your body. What do you see, hear, and feel? Where are you?

Next, visualize what your adult self looks and feels like now. Go to that place in time and rescue your inner child. Soothe the beliefs and fears that you had as a child. Maybe you felt abandoned or untrusting, and perhaps these feelings have lasted into your adult life. Imagine your adult self asking *your inner child what he/she needs*. In your visualization, take the child to a safe place.

Have a conversation with your inner child and ask what the child needs to feel safe and loved. It is about resolving the memory and changing it. *You can actually change the memories as they exist in your brain, and you can move forward with a different idea of who you are. If you can heal the feelings you had as a child, you can heal the underlying beliefs in your life as an adult.*

Have support from family, friends, or your therapist available after you complete this exercise because you may need to talk to someone supportive, especially if recalling a particularly traumatic incident.

There is an effective process called PNRT, Progressive Neuro Resolution Therapy, where a trained therapist can guide you and support you through this process. For more information, go to www.nicolemccance.com.

7 Tips to Help You Sleep

"Sometimes we need a little tears to clear the mist in our eyes, a little assurance to clear the doubts in our head, a little hug to nurse our aching heart, and a little rest to carry on and [move] forward"

—Islamic Thinking

Introduction: Sleep Tips

Sleep is often the first aspect of your life that is affected when you become depressed. You may find that you are sleeping too much or you might not be able to sleep for more than a few hours each night.

With just a few steps, you can change your sleep routine for the better. Once you feel well-rested, you can combat other issues that accompany depression. It may take a few weeks to establish healthy sleep patterns, and it might seem challenging at first, but good sleep hygiene is essential to restore your body and mind at night so you can function properly during the day.

If you find that you aren't getting restful sleep, try the tips offered in this section.

Quiet Anxious Thoughts Before Bed

It can be difficult to fall asleep when it seems that it's the only time during the day in which you have time to think. This time is often when all of the worry you had during the day accumulates, and you get caught up in a whirlwind of racing thoughts. How can you sleep if you're worrying? If you do manage to fall asleep after so much worrying, you may toss and turn, grind your teeth, or experience nightmares. You wake up not feeling rested at all. It is important to soothe your worries before trying to fall asleep.

Try This!

Set Aside a Time to Worry
This may seem strange, but setting aside 20 minutes to address your worries can be helpful. It isn't productive to worry at night when you are exhausted and not thinking clearly. Promise yourself that tomorrow, at a certain time, you will sit down and focus on the things that are bothering you. You may want to create a routine of reflecting in the same place, such as the car or shower. When tomorrow comes, you may find that your worry was irrational or unimportant. You might not even remember what was worrying you!

Planning
If there is a large issue that is bothering you, ask yourself what you can do about it and make a plan. Try to limit your worrying to solvable issues. If you are concerned about money and your worrying keeps you up at night, it could be because you are avoiding the issue

during the day. Address it by speaking to your bank, creditors, or a financial advisor. Open your mail and look at your bills—face the issues head on. Avoidance and denial only make worrying more severe.

Address Worrying

If you spend time worrying about irrational thoughts or unlikely scenarios such as worrying that your partner will leave you, ask yourself where this fear is coming from. Why are you so worried about this particular outcome? Ask yourself how your worrying can help the situation. Maybe you need to have an uncomfortable conversation with someone. Maybe you need to make some changes. More than likely, the worrying is acting as a distraction for another underlying issue, such as insecurity or not feeling in control.

Get Out of Your Head

Worrying usually exists in the mind, but it can often appear in the body in physical symptoms such as restlessness, body aches, headaches, digestive issues, muscle tension, difficulty breathing, and a racing heart. Next time you are lying in bed worrying, try to focus on your body instead of your mind. Review **Tip #3: Mindfulness in the Moment—Body Scanning Technique,** which is a simple breathing and body-focused exercise that you can do in bed, which will help let go of your worry and leave you feeling calm and relaxed. You can also download a free body-scanning audio at www.nicolemccance.com for a guided version of the tip.

 Tip #36

Light and Sleep

Imagine your bedroom. What does it look like at night? Is there always a television on while you sleep? Does light filter in from the hallway or bathroom? Is your alarm clock particularly bright? The smallest amount of light can alter your sleep patterns, preventing you from achieving full REM sleep. This in turn affects your body's ability to secrete the human growth hormone, which repairs and replenishes the body during the night.

Try This!

Turn off all lights and sleep in full darkness, and you will begin to feel more rested upon waking. Another option is purchasing an eye mask. Put this on when you sleep to block out even the smallest amount of light. The goal is to sleep in pitch black darkness. You will feel more rested and refreshed after following this simple tip.

Tip #37

Establishing a Routine

For both oversleeping and undersleeping, it is important to create a routine.

Try This!

Go to bed at the same time and get up at the same time whether or not you have somewhere to be in the morning. Set an alarm in the morning. If your body gets used to going to bed every night around the same time, it will be much easier to fall asleep as you have trained your body.

Try going to bed earlier. You must allow your body to progress through the stages of sleep, as you go through non-REM and REM cycles during the night. The earlier you fall asleep, the easier it is for your body to move through the many stages of sleep. Research shows the best quality of sleep happens between 10pm-2am. If you are asleep during this time, your body releases high amounts of the rejuvenating hormone, the human growth hormone. Going to bed earlier will have you feeling more rested in the morning and able to handle the stresses of the day.

Have a bedtime ritual. I suggest doing the same thing every night before bed. For example, make it a routine that you have a hot shower and then listen to a few minutes of soft music just before getting into bed. Some people enjoy lighting a candle and reading a few pages of a book or sipping warm milk. Because most of us are pretty wound up from the day, it's important to unwind with a ritual as it prepares your brain for sleep time. For a tip to incorporate into your bedtime routine refer to **Tip # 49: Aromatherapy for Depression.**

Natural Sleep Aids

These natural sleep aids should help ease your stress and allow you to feel calm at night. You should be able to achieve a more restful sleep after you find a remedy that works for you. You should check with your doctor before adding supplements to your daily routine if you have allergies or if you're taking any medications.

- Try taking a calcium/magnesium supplement. Calcium eases stress, nerves, muscle tension, and regulates mood. Magnesium helps to produce serotonin, which in turn produces melatonin, the chemical that helps to regulate your internal clock. Calcium and magnesium are best taken together, as they promote absorption in your body. Taking calcium and magnesium before bed helps to calm your mind and prepare you for a better sleep.

- A glass of warm milk will also give your body the calcium it needs for a good sleep. The milk alone may not do the trick, so take milk with a small amount of carbohydrates, such as a bowl of whole grain cereal. This carbohydrate, protein, tryptophan, and calcium snack will give you the right combination of sleep-triggering brain chemicals.

- Try drinking non-caffeinated tea before bed, such as lemon or chamomile.

- Valerian is a popular herb for promoting good sleep, as it stimulates relaxation in the body. It is available in many forms at health food stores, including tablets and teas.

Tips to Improve Your Nutrition

"You are what you eat."

—Dr. Victor Hugo Lindlahr
(American health food pioneer)

Serotonin and Tryptophan

Did you know that there is a natural pharmacy in your brain? You can gain access to positivity- releasing chemicals just by eating the right foods. This tip focuses on releasing the "happiness hormone," serotonin.

Serotonin is often referred to as the "happiness hormone," despite the fact that it is actually a neurotransmitter. It certainly does increase feelings of happiness, relaxation, and well-being. When our body releases serotonin, we experience the feeling that "everything is going to be all right." Our anxiety is eased, allowing us to sleep better, focus on tasks, and maintain a positive outlook on life.

So how do we release serotonin in our bodies? Tryptophan is the basis for conversion into serotonin.

Many proteins contain tryptophan (*you know, that amino acid that makes you feel sleepy after eating turkey*), and consuming foods rich in tryptophan will contribute to the release of serotonin.

Try This!

If you aren't eating these foods already, take a look at the list and see which ones you can easily incorporate into your diet.

Foods High in Tryptophan

Red Meat	Seaweed
Poultry	Fish
Seafood	Cheese
Milk (including soy milk)	Eggs
Dried dates	Parsley
Papaya	Onions
Mushrooms	Mustard greens and seeds
Watermelon	Celery
Squash	Carrots
Turnips & Rutabagas	Beets
Dried apricots	Sweet peppers

Sugar, Artificial Sweeteners, and Processed Foods

The brain depends on an even supply of nutrients throughout the day. This means eating a variety of healthy foods at regular intervals throughout the day.

Eating a diet of prepared and packaged food usually indicates a higher consumption of preservatives, artificial sweeteners, refined sugar, and carbohydrates. Many processed foods contain so much sugar that they cause a temporary high in mood and energy and a significant "crash" or decrease in mood and energy afterward. Regular intake of these stimulants creates an ongoing cycle of ups and downs. Diet soda and other products that contain the artificial sweetener aspartame have been linked to headaches, insomnia, and depression. This product can block the formation of serotonin which is needed to boost your mood. Processed food provides very little in the way of nutrients, meaning that **you are starving your brain of essential vitamins it needs to function and perform.**

Try to consume many **fresh vegetables and fruits** to receive the benefit of natural vitamins and sugars. Avoid refined carbohydrates such as white bread, rice, and pasta. There are so many healthy alternatives on the market that taste the same, if not better, than their unhealthy counterparts.

Try This!

If you are overwhelmed at the thought of researching and reading labels, follow the simple color rule while you are shopping and preparing meals. Cut out white foods (white bread, rice, pasta), and eat green and yellow foods (broccoli, spinach, squash, and other brightly colored vegetables), and brown foods (whole grain bread, potatoes, sweet potatoes, beans, etc.). Eat protein at each meal, whether it is from meat or another source.

Decreasing your sugar, sweetener, and processed food intake will improve your mood and provide you with other added health benefits. Even supplementing a granola bar with a piece of fruit is a good start!

Vitamin B

To achieve all the results that B vitamins have to offer, take a Complex B vitamin. B Vitamins have been proven to assist with the following:

- Emotional stress

- Depressed mood

- Cognitive functioning (concentration and memory)

- Nervous system functioning

- Energy

- Anxiety and panic attacks

- Sleep difficulty caused by restlessness and anxiety

The most important B vitamins for your mood are B12 and B9 (folate). If you wish to obtain these vitamins naturally, you can find folate (B9) in the following foods: fortified whole-grain breakfast cereals, lentils, black-eyed peas, soybeans, oatmeal, mustard greens, beets, broccoli, sunflower seeds, wheat germ, and oranges. Foods rich in vitamin B12: shellfish, wild salmon, fortified whole-grain breakfast cereal, lean beef, cottage cheese, yogurt, milk, and eggs. Next time you are at the grocery store, pick up at least two of these foods.

Omega 3[6, 7]

The human body requires Omega 3 fatty acids to function properly. The human brain is comprised of 60% fats, and approximately half of that fat is DHA Omega 3. This means that nature intended the human brain to be "powered" by fats. Functioning with a low supply of Omega 3s is somewhat like trying to run a car without fuel.

Deficiencies in Omega 3 fats have been linked to:

- Depression
- Anxiety
- Mood swings
- Bipolar disorder
- Postpartum depression
- Alzheimer's disease
- ADHD and ADD

Harvard researchers have shown some of these conditions will greatly improve with increased Omega 3 fatty acid intake. Other studies have shown that even if you don't have any of these conditions, memory and focus can improve with consistent use of fish oil supplements.

You can get Omega 3 oils from supplements, or you can incorporate Omega 3 into your diet by eating foods such as salmon, walnuts, and flax seeds. The recommended dosage varies based on your medical history and how much of this healthy fat you already consume in your diet. Consult with your doctor to determine if taking Omega 3 is right for you.

The bottom line is that Omega 3 helps your mind function, making it easier to process, understand, and recall information. There are also added benefits, such as glowing skin and hair!

Mindful Eating

Mindfulness is a psychological perspective that focuses on being in the moment and really connecting to the here and now. We talked about mindfulness in **Tip #3.** We can spend a lot of time thinking about the past and the uncertainties of the future, so mindfulness is a way of getting present to what is actually happening to you, rather than worrying about what may happen.

This mindful eating exercise can target a symptom of depression: overeating. We can often eat because it is something to do, to fill time. We begin to rely on food to comfort us and help us cope. When we overeat, we are not listening to our bodies. When you start to pay attention to your body and its connection to hunger, you are more likely to eat things that are healthier and to be satisfied with less than you would usually eat. When you consume healthy foods, your body's satiation response kicks in faster (this is the message that your stomach sends to your brain, saying, "I'm full"). You are satiated when you have absorbed the necessary nutrients to function. This is why it is so easy to mindlessly eat French fries and other nutrient-lacking foods. Despite satisfying your hunger, your body is still craving essential vitamins for functioning.

When we eat mindlessly, we are not paying attention to the basic needs of our bodies, or whether we are even hungry. Eat with your stomach and not your eyes. This means paying attention to the needs of your body and what it requires for energy, rather than eating things that simply look good and will satisfy your cravings. If you do have a craving for

chocolate or some other indulgence, purchase a treat with high-quality ingredients. (There are plenty of organic and even raw cacao products on the market that are rich and satisfying.) You can practice the following exercise when you buy a treat as well. It will stop you from eating an entire bag of chips or cookies, or finishing a chocolate bar without noticing.

Try This!

Complete this exercise at your next meal:

- Stop and sit, with the intent to eat your meal. Do not watch television, read, or do anything besides eating your meal.
- With each bite, try to not only eat your food, but *experience* it. Be aware of the texture and taste of the food. Be aware of all of the sensations in your body during this experience.
- Become aware of the restorative nature of food, and feel your stomach becoming full.
- Eat slowly and take smaller bites. Chew your food completely before swallowing it.
- Do not try to finish what is on your plate. Instead, stop eating when your stomach communicates to your brain that you are full.

Mind/Body Tips

"Each morning, we are born again; what we do today, is what matters most."

—Buddha

Light Therapy for Seasonal Depression

If your sadness tends to intensify in the winter months, you may be suffering from Seasonal Affective Disorder (SAD). During the winter months, when it is dark later in the mornings and earlier in the evenings, and we spend the majority of time indoors in low light, we can develop symptoms of depression. The most popular theory for the cause of SAD is that the lack of natural light in the winter upsets our body's natural rhythm. Without as much sunlight, our body's natural release of neurotransmitters that regulate sleep, mood, and appetite are disturbed. SAD symptoms can include fatigue, irritability, appetite changes, lack of motivation, anxiety, avoidance of social contact, and general sadness.

There is treatment available for this condition. While psychotherapy is beneficial for all kinds of depression, SAD is a very specific type of mood disorder than can be treated with light therapy. Studies have found that light therapy is just as effective in treating SAD as the use of anti-depressants. Those who were treated with light therapy showed greater improvement in their symptoms in one week than those who took anti-depressants.

Light therapy works by emitting 10,000 lux of light (which is equivalent to outdoor light on a bright day), which soothes your body's craving for sunshine. In turn, your depressive symptoms should subside. Light boxes to treat

SAD are widely available for purchase online and at major drug stores. Some side effects can occur with the use of a light box, such as headaches and dizziness. If these symptoms occur, a lower dose of light is recommended.

This tip is not intended to diagnose Seasonal Affective Disorder. If you feel that you may be suffering from it, consult your family doctor before pursuing any form of treatment, including light box therapy.

Natural High: Release Endorphins for Stress and Pain

Endorphins are chemicals released by the brain that give you a natural sense of well-being. They act much like opiates, such as morphine or oxycodone, in that they can provide feelings of euphoria, when an individual experiences an "endorphin rush." A large release of endorphins can be brought about by prolonged, intense exercise. Runners often experience "runner's high," in which their brain is flooded with endorphins and other feel-good chemicals, dulling any pain they might be experiencing and allowing them to happily continue their run.

Endorphins are released when you:

- Fall in love
- Exercise
- Have sex
- Eat chocolate
- Eat chili peppers
- Get a massage or acupuncture treatment
- Practice yoga and meditation

Try This!

Try engaging in endorphin-releasing activities to access the natural chemicals your brain has to offer. When endorphins are released into the brain, stress, anxiety, and pain are momentarily dulled, allowing you to focus on being positive and possibly make certain changes for lasting happiness.

Exercise

Regular exercise promotes better sleep, promotes better eating habits, and elevates your mood. Exercise also stimulates mental functioning and releases feel-good brain chemicals, dopamine, and endorphins. The key is to get up and get your whole body moving (or if you cannot do that, move whatever you can). It doesn't have to be in a gym; it could be gardening or any other exercise of your choice.

Exercise helps to prevent and improve many physical health problems. The link between anxiety, depression, and exercise is not entirely clear; but studies consistently show that individuals who exercise have better psychological and physical health. Exercise also serves as a stress-reliever and helps you to relax. Exercising on a consistent basis gives you lasting energy throughout the day.

We all struggle with the motivation to go for a walk or a run or to the gym, but exercise is such an important part of our lives that it's worth getting out of bed in the morning and leaving the house—or simply stepping on that treadmill. We often tell ourselves that we will go to the gym tomorrow because we are too tired today. However, if you *start changing the way you think about exercise*, it will become easier to make it a part of your routine.

What if you were to tell yourself that if you DON'T go to the gym, you will be tired all day. This new thought could motivate you because the pain of being tired all day is more motivating then the pain of getting to the gym. If you tell

yourself this enough times, you will start to believe it and it will become a habit to get to the gym before work, as you would have felt the difference in your energy all day.

Act as if exercise is a part of your day, just like showering, eating, and brushing your teeth. Treat exercise just like medicine for your mood and your body. It will promote physical health and help you combat stress, anxiety, lethargy, and depression.

Try This!

Make a plan to exercise and have a friend or trainer hold you accountable. Start making exercise an important part of your day.

You can incorporate exercise into your day right now by completing the next tip, **Stretches for the Body and Mind.**

Stretches for the Body and Mind[8,9]

Yoga poses and stretches are restorative for your body as well as your mind. Many of us rest only during sleep, but it is important to calm the mind in our waking hours. The Mayo Clinic endorses yoga as being effective in stress reduction and increased fitness, and they suggest it for the management of chronic health conditions including insomnia, fatigue, cancer, and chronic pain disorders.

Sadness can often manifest itself in physical symptoms so that those suffering from depression display slumped shoulders, sunken chests, or stiffness throughout the body. While getting in touch with that sadness, an individual may discover that those negative feelings are actually carried in a physical location such as the neck, back, or shoulders. Practicing yoga for a few minutes each day, or even a few times per week, will help to ease your depressive symptoms. You don't have to join a gym or a yoga class to complete basic stretches at home, as I recommend a few of them in this tip. If you begin these stretches and find them enjoyable as well as beneficial, yoga classes are offered at most wellness facilities, or there are a number of videos available to guide you through your practice.*

---

*As with all new exercise regimens, do not push yourself past your physical limit and consult your family physician regarding any medical issues that may conflict with the poses suggested here.

Try This!**

Legs up the Wall

This pose is very simple and should not stress or strain your body in any way. It is helpful in releasing pain in the body, as well as increasing circulation to the brain, pelvis, and heart. It is particularly effective in relieving headaches and anxiety.

Note: Using a support under your lower back may be helpful in this pose. This support may be a yoga block, a pillow, or a rolled-up blanket. Place the support under your lower back, just above the buttocks.

○ Position your yoga mat perpendicular to the wall. Sit down on your yoga mat, facing the wall. You may turn slightly to either side, as you lie down and raise your legs up straight, against the wall.

○ You will notice that tension in your back and legs eases, and your mind will begin to relax.

○ Stay in this position from 1–10 minutes.

**To complete the following poses, you will need a yoga mat for your safety and comfort.

Downward Facing Dog

This pose is probably the most recognized yoga stretch, and is important for many reasons. It has wonderful mental relaxation properties, as well as physically strengthening your muscles and limbs. It is a great whole-body stretch that is simple and approachable for most beginners.

- On the mat, lower yourself onto your hands and knees. Place your knees directly below your hips. Your hands should be positioned in front of your shoulders. Spread your fingers and turn your toes under to support yourself, as you gently and slowly lift your knees up and away from your mat, pulling your body in an arched position above the mat.

- Exhaling, reach your buttocks toward the ceiling while pushing your heels downward. Straighten your upper body as your heels lower. Your heels do not have to touch the ground, but as they get closer to reaching the ground, you will achieve the deepest stretch in your legs.

- Tuck your head so that it is parallel to your shoulders.

- Feel this deep stretch. Hold for 1 to 3 minutes, breathing deeply. With each exhalation, move your body into a deeper stretch.

Seated Twist

This pose helps to cleanse and massage the liver. The liver is thought to have over 500 functions within the human body, and it works in combination with other organs to keep you healthy.

- Sit on your mat in a cross-legged position.
- Place your right hand on the floor beside your body, and twist your upper body to the right.

- Turn your head to look over your right shoulder.
- Hold this pose for 2 deep breaths, or 10 seconds, and return to the center.
- Repeat this turn on your left side.

Acupuncture for Depression[10, 11, 12, 13, 14, 15]

Many people seek alternatives to anti-depressants for the treatment of depression. Western medicine relies on psychotherapy and anti-depressants to overcome depression, while Traditional Chinese Medicine (also referred to as TCM) views emotions as connected to the physical body, and vice versa. The aim of Chinese medicine is to balance the mind and body as an interconnected system.

Studies have shown that acupuncture can be effective in the treatment of depression. One study concluded that acupuncture may positively alter the brain's chemistry through the release of hormones and neurotransmitters. Acupuncture is also promising in the treatment of pregnant and menopausal women. Recent Chinese studies have concluded that acupuncture is as effective as anti-depressant medication but produces no adverse side effects.

Chinese medicine approaches depression differently to each individual and targets specific patterns of symptoms. Symptoms of depression will most likely fall under two main categories: either deficiency (qi) or excess (yin).

Deficiency

Emotional symptoms such as worry and anxiety may be present. Physical symptoms will include loss of appetite and weight, sleep difficulties, fatigue, and concentration and memory issues.

Excess

Emotional symptoms can include irritability, anger, reactivity, and agitation. Physical symptoms include dizziness, fatigue, and weight gain.

An individual may carry symptoms from both categories. Chinese medicine includes acupuncture and herbal remedies. Acupuncture practitioners take the time to discuss both you as an individual and your symptoms. Traditional medicine would prescribe the same treatment for different individuals with similar symptoms, but Chinese medicine treats people and their bodies as unique.

Try This!

Search locally or consult the American Association of Acupuncture & Oriental Medicine to find a reputable acupuncturist in your area. Set up appointments for a few acupuncture sessions (many health insurance companies approve acupuncture treatments) and experience the benefits!

Aromatherapy for Depression[16,17]

Aromatherapy is a remedy that uses essential oils to stimulate beneficial change in the body. Researchers are not entirely sure how essential oils produce such positive effects, but it is thought that the receptors in your nose communicate with specific parts of the brain, producing activity that promotes physical and emotional health. For example, some scientists believe that the scent of lavender creates the same brain activity that is produced from the use of sedative medication.

Essential oils are extracted from flowers, leaves, or grasses using the process of steam distillation. These oils are especially useful in the treatment of stress-related and emotional disorders. Essential oils are very concentrated, so it is important to dilute them and only use a drop or two. Oils may be used in a bath, after a shower, or used with a massage. Essential oils can irritate the skin; therefore dilute oils with a scent-free cream, oil, or lotion before applying directly to the skin. They may also be inhaled, and special aromatherapy vaporizers are widely available.

You can tailor your aromatherapy routine to the way you are feeling right now. Regular use of aromatherapy can ease depression, anxiety, and stress. You can purchase essential oils at most health food stores.

Essential Oils that Combat Depression:

Bergamot	Lavender
Myrrh	Neroli
Patchouli	Peppermint
Thyme	Chamomile
Elemi	Frankincense
Geranium	Jasmine

Lavender and Chamomile are especially helpful in promoting sound sleep, which helps to ease depressive symptoms. Add a drop or two of the selected essential oil to a cotton ball and place near your bed at night. Alternatively, lightly mist your sheets with a dilution of water and essential oil. Keep in mind that you must enjoy the scent for it to be effective, rather than it being distracting to you. Sample a few essential oils until you find a few that work for you.

Try This!

Incorporate aromatherapy into your daily shower, bath, or bedtime routine.

Bach Flower Remedies

This type of remedy was developed by Dr. Edward Bach in the early 1900s. The main belief of his treatment system is that physical illness is a manifestation of underlying emotional distress. He sought to restore emotional balance through the use of gentle, effective essences of flowers. These flower remedies are ingested in a diluted form. Add a drop of the remedy to spring water and sip over a period of a few hours.

The most popular remedy is called Rescue Remedy. It can be purchased online, and it is available pre-mixed in many health food stores and homeopathic pharmacies, all at minimal cost. Rescue Remedy is used to alleviate any form of stress from extreme crisis to slight anxiety. It is particularly effective in situations where you feel completely overwhelmed, hopeless, or frustrated. According to Dr. Bach, you don't have to know the cause of your feelings because the remedy targets your emotions and heals your distress.

Several other flower remedies can be used alone or in combination with a few other essences to target specific symptoms of depression.

Agrimony — This remedy targets your underlying anguish as you put on a brave face to the world. It soothes your internal suffering.

Cerato — Cerato addresses your need for affirmation from others and your low self-esteem. Take this remedy if you are lacking interest and are withdrawn.

Elm — Useful if you have the negative belief that you are incompetent. You feel that you

cannot do anything right and may believe that you will never accomplish your goals.

Gorse	Gorse is a flower remedy that eases feelings of despair, usually occurring as a result of a trauma. Take this if you are worrying that your life will never return to normal and you cannot see past a traumatic event such as a death, divorce, or other significant loss.
Mustard	Mustard is effective in easing general sadness and sorrow.
Red Chestnut	A prevalent symptom of depression is worry. If you worry constantly and experience excessive concern in your own life, as well as the lives of your friends and family, red chestnut remedy will alleviate this pervasive worry.
Rock Rose	This remedy targets irrational fears and beliefs. It is especially useful in treating terrifying nightmares.
Sweet Chestnut	If you feel alone and alienated from others, this is a soothing remedy that will relieve your anguish.
White Chestnut	Taken for obsessive thoughts, this remedy is helpful if you fixate or dwell on a certain idea.

Try This!

Choosing a remedy requires a certain amount of reflection on your own emotions. Bach remedies are effective only once you pinpoint your symptoms. Read the symptoms above carefully, then create a list of how you are feeling right now and rate each item on the list of emotions on a scale of 1–10. Target the most intense feelings first. The Bach Flower Remedies are most effective when taken in minimal combinations (no more than 5 are recommended). The Bach Flower Remedies are an effective, safe, and natural way to treat symptoms of depression, and can be found in most natural food stores.

Orgasm to Happiness[18,19,20]

Practicing self-care is important for all of us, especially for those suffering from depression. When we are depressed, we can lose a sense of self-worth and stop caring about our health and wellness. Eating well, exercising, and taking care of our needs is important in recovering from depression. Another aspect of self-care is satisfying our sexual needs. This is important to do whether we are married, in a relationship, or single. Sexual stimulation, leading to orgasm, is a simple way to access the feel-good chemicals in the brain.

When we crave sex, we are craving the dopamine, oxytocin, and other chemicals that are released during orgasm.

Why is an Orgasm So Good for You?

- In the moments before an orgasm, a flood of oxytocin is released. Oxytocin is often referred to as the "love hormone" because it is released during touching, hugging, and orgasms, and is present in higher amounts in those who are falling in love. Oxytocin helps us to feel calm, relaxed, and safe. It also inhibits the release of cortisol, the stress hormone.

- Endorphins, which are natural mood-boosters and stress-relievers, are also released.

- Every time you reach orgasm, hormone levels of DHEA increase. DHEA boosts your immune system, improves cognition, keeps skin healthy, and even works as an antidepressant. It is also known as the "anti-aging" hormone.

Try This!

It may seem like a strange prescription, but I recommend having orgasms 3–5 times per week in order to boost your mood, feel more relaxed and calm, think more clearly, and counteract the symptoms of depression. Engage in sexual activity with a partner or self-pleasure to achieve an orgasm, and feel better!

Releasing Bodily-Felt Emotions

Depression tends to cause ruminating, obsessive thoughts, where we become stuck in a negative thought pattern. This exercise assists in releasing you from the grip of these thoughts, as it is a process that draws you into your body.

Our memories are stored in our brain, and we are able to recall past events by remembering. However, there is another type of memory that stays in the body and can be brought up involuntarily. Many people who are depressed hold their sadness in various parts of their body at the cellular level. A sound, touch, smell, taste, or sight may trigger a bodily reaction, but not thoughts from your brain. Your body may tense up or elicit pain. Your body is saying, "I don't like that. I remember that." This is a bodily flashback that your brain may not have access to.

The following process helps you to release whatever emotions, memories, and trauma you are holding in your body.

Try This!

Lie down, close your eyes, and focus on your breathing. Let your breathing go to a part of your body where you feel tightness, discomfort, or tension. Does this physical feeling cause you to experience any emotional response? Do you feel a knot in your stomach? What emotion or image or memory comes to mind as you focus on this knot? Is the heaviness you feel in your chest connected to anxiety? This process may take some practice, so keep trying.

Now, breathe into the area and relax that part of your body. Feel and visualize the emotional baggage leaving, like a weight being lifted. Imagine that each breath you take in is traveling straight to that part of your body; and with each breath out, the emotional pain is leaving your body. You may even want to visualize yourself inhaling a soothing, healing color and exhaling a different color as you release the toxic emotion. By letting the pain go, you are healing that emotional and physical part of you.

Congratulations!

I am sure this has been a journey for you. You have learned new ways of thinking, acting, eating, breathing, and may have even tried holistic remedies!

How do you feel? Do you feel different than before you started doing the exercises and using the tools in this book?

The thing about your mood, depression in particular, is that it can come and go. You now have the coping skills to handle depression; you are now better prepared to manage it and even beat it. My hope is that the dark cloud has lifted and you are on your way to a more fulfilling, content, and happy life.

Appendix

Additional Tools

How Are You Feeling?

*A*fter you've tried a majority of the tips in this book, over a period of 30 days or more, track your progress using the self-assessment on the following page and compare your symptoms to how you felt when you began using the tips.

52 Ways to Beat Depression *Naturally*

Symptoms of Clinical Depression

Self-Assessment   Date: _____

Yes No

☐ ☐ Do you feel depressed or sad for most of the day, or every day?

☐ ☐ Have you lost interest in all or almost all of the activities you used to enjoy?

☐ ☐ Have you lost or gained a significant amount of weight, or has your appetite changed dramatically?

☐ ☐ Do you often have trouble sleeping, or do you sleep all the time?

☐ ☐ Do you feel restless or agitated frequently?

☐ ☐ Is your energy level low and/or do you feel fatigued?

☐ ☐ Do you have feelings of inadequacy, loss of self-esteem, and/or do you put yourself down?

☐ ☐ Do you have trouble concentrating, paying attention, or thinking clearly?

☐ ☐ Do you have recurring thoughts of death or suicide or sometimes wish you were dead?

Suggested Schedules

Below are 3 suggested schedules of how to incorporate the tips easily into your daily life. Feel free to create your own routine or try one of these. Soon they will become new positive uplifting habits. You may want to try these schedules with a friend and share your success at the end of the day.

Suggested Schedule #1

1. Wake up at a set time. (Tip #37)
2. Eat a good breakfast with eggs and meat or whole-grain cereal with milk and fruit. Eat mindfully. (Tip #40, 41, 42, 43)
3. Complete the Smile Exercise. (Tip #13)
4. Go about your usual day (commute, work, errands, etc.) while using the Rubber Band Technique to work on negative thinking patterns. (Tip #14)
5. Get outside for a walk at lunchtime or in the afternoon. If inclined, exercise or do yoga instead. (Tip #9, 45, 46, 47)
6. Have a good dinner, preferably vegetables with salmon or red meat. (Tip #39, 40)
7. Complete the Gratitude Exercise. (Tip #31)
8. Go to bed at a set time. (Tip #37)

Suggested Schedule #2

1. Wake up at set time. (Tip #37)
2. Do the Gratitude Exercise while going about morning routine. (Tip #31)
3. Take Vitamin B. (Tip # 41)
4. Throughout the day, do the Thought Stopping Technique. (Tip #23)
5. Use Tapping To Calm You when needed throughout day. (Tip #5)
6. Go outside for a walk at lunch. (Tip #9, 46)
7. Call a friend when you get home. (Tip #12)
8. Take a calcium supplement before bed. (Tip #38)
9. Reframe your depressed thinking while in bed with a journal. (Tip #19)
10. Do breathing exercises before bed. (Tip #1 or 35)

Suggested Schedule #3

1. Wake up at set time. (Tip #37).
2. Use SAD lamp. (Tip #44)
3. Take bach flower remedy. (Tip #50)
4. Take vitamins (vitamin b and omega 3). (Tip # 41, 42)
5. Go for a walk. (Tip #9, 46)
6. Practice thought stopping. (Tip #23)
7. Practice changing focus throughout day. (Tip #22)
8. Go for acupuncture. (Tip #48)
9. Reflect on your day. (Tip #28)
10. Take a calcium supplement before bed. (Tip #38)
11. Create a bedtime routine (take a bath, listen to music, read, use aromatherapy). (Tip #37, 49).

Activity Diary

Worksheet for Tip #7: Behavioral Activation

Track your activity, rest, thoughts, and mood using the chart on the next page. Copy this chart into your journal or create a template on your computer to print out. I recommend tracking your activity and mood for at least one week. You may notice that your mood spikes upward when you spend time with your family or when you get out of the house, as your mood tends to increase when you engage in activity, rather than being sedentary. The activity diary will allow you to see patterns in your mood and notice the peaks and valleys throughout the day. With this information, you will become aware of the activities you do and how they impact your mood. In turn, you will have more control over how you feel throughout the day.

Example:

Time	Activity	Mood/Emotion Rate intensity of mood (0–100%)
7am – 9am	Stayed in bed thinking about all the things I have to do today and what I didn't get done yesterday	Anxiety 50% Depressed 70% Dread 60% Guilt 60%

Date:		Mood/Emotion
		Rate intensity of mood (0–100%)
Time	Activity	
7am – 9am		
9am – 11am		
11am – 1pm		
1pm – 3pm		
3pm – 5pm		
5pm – 7pm		
7pm – 9pm		
9pm – 11pm		

References

Tip #6: Meditation for Depression

1. University of Massachusetts, *Center for Mindfulness: The Stress Reduction Program,* http://www.umassmed.edu/Content.aspx-?id=41254, 2012.
2. D. S. Khalsa and C. Stauth, *Meditation as Medicine,* (Simon and Shuster, 2001).

Tip #8: Bring the Outside In & Tip #9: Get Outside

3. R. M. Ryan, et al., "Vitalizing Effects of Being Outdoors and in Nature," *Journal of Environmental Psychology,* 2010:30(2):159.

Tip #31: Gratitude Exercise

4. R. A. Emmons and M. E. McCullough, "Counting Blessings Versus Burdens: Experimental Studies of Gratitude and Subjective Well-Being in Daily Life," *Journal of Personality and Social Psychology,* 84:377–389.
5. J. Froh, W. J. Sefick, and R. A. Emmons, "Counting Blessings in Early Adolescents: An Experimental Study of Gratitude and Subjective Well-Being. *Journal of School Psychology, 2008:46*:213–233.

Tip#42: Omega 3

6. A. L. Stoll, et al., "Omega-3 Fatty Acids in Bipolar Disorder: A Preliminary Double-Blind, Placebo-Controlled Trial," *Archives Gen Psychiatry,* 1999:56:407–412.
7. A. L. Stoll, et al., "Methodological Considerations in Clinical Studies of Omega-3 Fatty Acids in Major Depression and Bipolar Disorder." *World Rev Nutr Diet,* 2000.

Tip #47: Stretches for the Body and Mind

8. Mayo Clinic, "Yoga: Tap into the many health benefits," 2012, http://www.mayoclinic.com/health/yoga/CM00004.
9. T. McCall, "Yoga for Depression, Part 1," *Yoga Journal.* http://www.yogajournal.com/for_teachers/2426?page=2.

Tip #48: Acupuncture for Depression

10. J. Allen, R. Schnyer, and S. Hitt, "The Efficacy of Acupuncture in the Treatment of Major Depressive Disorder in Women," *Psychol. Sci.* 1998:9:397–401.

11. R. Manber, J. Allen, and M. Morris, "Alternative Treatments for Depression: Empirical Support and Relevance to Women," *J. Clin. Psychiatry,* 2002:63(7):628–40.

12. G. Porzio, T. Trapasso, and S. Martelli, et al., "Acupuncture in the Treatment of Menopause-Related Symptoms in Women Taking Tamoxifen," *Tumori,* 2002:88:12–130.

13. J. Han, "Electroacupuncture: An Alternative to Antidepressants for Treating Affective Diseases?" *Int J Neurosci* 1986:29:79–92.

14. C. Han, X. Li, H. Luo, X. Zhao, and X. Li, "Clinical Study on Electro-Acupuncture Treatment for 30 Cases of Mental Depression, *J Tradit Chin Med.* 2004:24(3):172–176.

15. H. Luo, F. Meng, Y. Jia, and X. Zhao, "Clinical Research on the Therapeutic Effect of the Electro-Acupuncture in Patients with Depression," *Psychiatry Clinical Neuroscience,* 1998:52:S338–340.

Tip #49: Aromatherapy for Depression

16. J. Zand, A. Spreen, and J. LaValle, *Smart Medicine for Healthier Living.* (New York: Avery).

17. University of Maryland Medical Center, 2012, http://www.umm.edu/altmed/articles/aromatherapy-000347.htm.

Tip #51: Orgasm to Happiness

18. T. DeAngelis, "The Two Faces of Oxytocin," *Monitor on Psychology*, February 2008: Vol 39 (2), http://www.apa.org/monitor/feb08/oxytocin.aspx.

19. Psych Central, 2012, "About Oxytocin," http://psychcentral.com/lib/2008/about-oxytocin/all/1/.

20. N. Turner, 2001, "More Sex is the Secret to a Longer Healthier Life," *Chatelaine*, http://www.chatelaine.com/en/article/24139—more-sex-is-the-secret-to-a-longer-healthier-life.

Acknowledgements

*I*t takes more than one person to write a book. In order for this book to materialize, I was supported by some amazing people. First and foremost, I would like to thank Amanda Paterson for her superb research and editing skills which helped this book get out into the world for people to read.

I would also like to thank Angie Doyle for making sure the administrative side of my practice ran smoothly while I concentrated on the book. Thanks for your unwavering commitment to my practice and my clients.

To my lovely friends for their encouragement along the way and for taking the time to review the book: I could not have done it without you.